C000172961

Ibsen's

A NEW VERSION BY FRANK McGUINNESS

Henrik Ibsen (1828–1906), Norwegian poet and
playwright, was one of the shapers of modern theatre,
who tempered naturalism with an understanding of
social responsibility and individual psychology. His
earliest major plays, *Brand* (1866) and *Peer Gynt* (1867),
were large-scale verse dramas, but with *Pillars of the
Community* (1877) he began to explore contemporary
issues. There followed *A Doll's House* (1879), *Ghosts*
(1881) and *An Enemy of the People* (1882). A richer
understanding of the complexity of human impulses
marks such later works as *The Wild Duck* (1885),
Rosmersholm (1886), *Hedda Gabler* (1890) and *The
Master Builder* (1892), while the imminence of mortality
overshadows his last great plays, *John Gabriel Borkman*
(1896) and *When We Dead Awaken* (1899).

Frank McGuinness was born in Buncrana, Co. Donegal,
and now lives in Dublin and lectures in English at
University College Dublin. His plays include *The Factory
Girls* (1982), *Baglady* (1985), *Observe the Sons of Ulster
Marching Towards the Somme* (1985), *Innocence* (1986),
Carthaginians (1988), *Mary and Lizzie* (1989), *The Bread
Man* (1991), *Someone Who'll Watch Over Me* (1992),
The Bird Sanctuary (1994), *Mutabilitie* (1997), *Dolly
West's Kitchen* (1999), *Gates of Gold* (2002), *Speaking
Like Magpies* (2005), *There Came a Gypsy Riding* (2007)
and *Greta Garbo Came to Donegal* (2010). Among his
many widely staged versions are Ibsen's *Rosmersholm*
(1987), *Peer Gynt* (1988), *Hedda Gabler* (1994), *A Doll's
House* (1997), and *The Lady from the Sea* (2008).

also by Frank McGuinness

GATES OF GOLD
DOLLY WEST'S KITCHEN
MARY AND LIZZIE
SOMEONE WHO'LL WATCH OVER ME
MUTABILITIE
OBSERVE THE SONS OF ULSTER MARCHING TOWARDS THE SOMME
SPEAKING LIKE MAGPIES
THERE CAME A GYPSY RIDING
GRETA GARBO CAME TO DONEGAL

FRANK McGUINNESS PLAYS ONE
(*The Factory Girls,
Observe the Sons of Ulster Marching Towards the Somme,
Innocence, Carthaginians, Baglady*)

FRANK McGUINNESS PLAYS TWO
(*Mary and Lizzie, Someone Who'll Watch Over Me,
Dolly West's Kitchen, The Bird Sanctuary*)

Translations
A DOLL'S HOUSE (Ibsen)
PEER GYNT (Ibsen)
ELECTRA (Sophocles)
OEDIPUS (Sophocles)
THE STORM (Ostrovsky)
HECUBA (Euripides)
MISS JULIE (Strindberg)
PHAEDRA (Racine)
THE LADY FROM THE SEA (Ibsen)
HELEN (Euripides)

Screenplays
Brian Friel's DANCING AT LUGHNASA

THE DAZZLING DARK: NEW IRISH PLAYS
(edited by Frank McGuinness)

HENRIK IBSEN

Ghosts

a version by
Frank McGuinness

from a literal translation by
Charlotte Barslund

faber and faber

First published in 2010
by Faber and Faber Limited
74–77 Great Russell Street, London WC1B 3DA

Typeset by Country Setting, Kingsdown, Kent CT14 8ES
Printed in England by CPI Bookmarque, Croydon, Surrey

A CIP record for this book
is available from the British Library

ISBN 978-0-571-26002-7

2 4 6 8 10 9 7 5 3

For John and Kaye Fanning

Ghosts, in this version by Frank McGuinness, was first performed at the Bristol Old Vic on 30 January 2007. The cast, in alphabetical order, was as follows:

Regine Séainin Brennan
Oswald Sam Crane
Pastor Manders Simon Shepherd
Engstrand John Stahl
Mrs Alving Sian Thomas

Director Robert Bowman
Designer Tom Piper
Lighting Ben Ormerod
Sound and Music Jason Barnes

Ghosts, in this version by Frank McGuinness, was first performed in London at the Duchess Theatre on 11 February 2010. The cast, in alphabetical order, was as follows:

Pastor Manders Iain Glen
Regine Jessica Raine
Mrs Alving Lesley Sharp
Engstrand Malcolm Storry
Oswald Harry Treadaway

Director Iain Glen
Designer Stephen Brimson Lewis
Lighting Oliver Fenwick
Sound and Music Richard Hammarton
Associate Director Amelia Sears

Characters

Mrs Helene Alving
Captain Alving's widow

Oswald Alving
her son, a painter

Pastor Manders

Engstrand
a carpenter

Regine Engstrand
in Mrs Alving's service

The action takes place on Mrs Alving's
country estate by a large fjord in Western Norway

GHOSTS

Act One

*A large garden room. Stage left, there is a door on the
wall. Stage right, there are two doors on the wall. There
is a circular table, surrounded by chairs, in the middle
of the room. Books, magazines and newspapers lie on
the table. There is a window downstage left. Next to it
is a small sofa with a work table in front of it. Upstage
the room stretches into an open, somewhat smaller
conservatory with walls of glass and large windows.
On the right-hand side of the conservatory a door leads
down to the garden.*

*The landscape of a fjord, secretive, shrouded by rain
that falls continuously, can be barely seen through the
glass walls.*

*Engstrand, a carpenter, stands by the garden door.
His left leg is a little bent. He has fitted a wooden block
to the sole of his boot.*

*Holding an empty flower spray, Regine prevents him
from coming any closer. She lowers her voice.*

Regine What are you looking for? Stay put where you
are. You're soaking wet.

Engstrand Daughter, it's the Lord above who sends this
rain.

Regine No, the Devil does – that's who sends it.

Engstrand Jesus, the things you come out with, Regine.

He limps a few steps into the living room.

All I'm here to say is –

Regine Make less noise with that hoof. The master is upstairs in his bed.

Engstrand Still snoozing? The morning's come and gone.

Regine No concern of yours.

Engstrand I downed a few drinks last night.

Regine You don't surprise me.

Engstrand Daughter, we'll all human, we err –

Regine We do, yes.

Engstrand This world is full of temptations – you know yourself. Still, I was at my work by half past five this morning, as God is my witness.

Regine Yes, yes. Now get on your way. I can't stand here and engage in rendezvous with you.

Engstrand What?

Regine I want nobody seeing you here. Go away.

He takes a few steps closer.

Engstrand No, by Christ, I'm not budging till you and me have had a word. I'll finish my work down at the school this afternoon, then I'm back on the boat to the town tonight.

Regine mutters.

Regine May God go with you.

Engstrand Thank you, daughter. They'll bless the opening of the orphanage tomorrow, and strong drink will be flowing. Let no man say Jacob Engstrand can't control himself in the face of temptation.

Regine Yes.

Engstrand Yes, indeed, because all the swanks will show their faces tomorrow. They're expecting Pastor Manders from the town.

Regine He's coming here today.

Engstrand What did I tell you? I'm damned if I'm letting him mark me down, do you understand?

Regine So that's what this is all in aid of.

Engstrand What?

She looks at him knowingly.

Regine What fast one are you going to pull on that man this time?

Engstrand Me try anything on Pastor Manders? Not at all. He's been too kind to me to try any trick like that. No, I wanted to talk to you about why I am going back tonight.

Regine The sooner I see the back of you the better.

Engstrand Regine, I want to take you with me.

She answers with open mouth.

Regine You want to take me? – Have I heard right?

Engstrand You, Regine. Back with me. That's what I'm saying.

Regine There's more chance of the world ending than me setting foot on that boat with you.

Engstrand Is there? We'll see about that.

Regine You can rest assured. I've grown used to gentry. Mrs Alving nearly treats me like one of the family. Why move bag and baggage in with you? In a house like that? Have sense.

5

Engstrand What in hell's name is this? Are you squaring up against your father, girl?

She mutters without looking at him.

Regine You've often repeated I was nothing to you.

Engstrand Fool's talk – don't listen to that –

Regine Wasn't it you who roared at me, calling me – *Fi donc!*

Engstrand I never used language like that – I swear –

Regine I know the kind of language you used.

Engstrand I was not well – my nerves. Regine, this world is full of temptations.

Regine snorts.

I did it when your mother was upsetting me. I had to find some way to annoy her back. She was always full of airs and graces.

He mimics.

'Set me free, Engstrand. Let me go. I served the Chamberlain. I served Monsieur Alving. I served him for three years at Rosenvold.' 'Monsieur', Jesus. Chamberlain.

He laughs.

He got his title when she was in service there and she never forgot it.

Regine Poor Mama – you soon drove her into an early grave.

He is uneasy.

Engstrand All my fault – is it? I see.

She turns away, barely audible.

Regine Dirty peg-leg.

Engstrand What did you say, daughter?

Regine *Pied de mouton.*

Engstrand Are you speaking in English?

Regine I am.

Engstrand Good, you've studied well out here. That will be useful now, Regine.

Silence.

Regine Why do you want me in the town?

Engstrand You've to ask why a father wants his only daughter? Am I not a lonely forsaken widower?

Regine Save me that sob story. Why do you want me in the town?

Engstrand All right, if you let me, I'll tell you. I have a new trick up my sleeve.

Regine Same old sleeve, same old trick.

Engstrand All I wanted to report is that I've put aside a decent bit of money from my work at the new orphanage here.

Regine Have you? How delightful for you.

Engstrand What else is there to spend money on in this place?

Regine Nothing. So, carry on?

Engstrand Well, you know yourself, I had the idea of investing the money into something that would make more money back. Sailors – a sort of canteen for –

Regine Sailors –

Engstrand A respectable place, honest to God – nice – not some pigsty. Nothing like that. Captains, officers, the best of people, honest to God. It would cater –

Regine And I would cater for –

Engstrand You would muck in – you'd help – for the sake of appearance – you understand. You'd have a fine life, my girl, easy. You can do exactly as you please.

Regine Is that so?

Engstrand The place will need a woman's touch. Definitely. Clear as daylight. In the evenings the lads will want singing, dancing, singing, dancing. You have to realise these boys have been wandering on the seven seas. You must appreciate that.

He moves closer.

Are you going to stand in your own way, Regine? Are you that stupid? What can you make of yourself out here? So Mrs Alving has spent money educating you – what good is that? From what I hear you are in charge of the youngsters at the new orphanage. Is that you? Will you work your fingers to the bone for those dirty bastards?

Regine That's not what I wanted, no. Who can say? Anything can happen.

Engstrand What can happen?

Regine Never you mind. How much money have you saved?

Engstrand About seven – eight hundred kroner.

Regine Enough, not bad.

Engstrand Enough to give us a start, girl.

Regine Were you not thinking of handing me some of that money?

Engstrand No, I was not thinking of that. Damned if I was.

Regine A dress maybe – a little something to make a new dress.

Engstrand Come with me, daughter, and you'll be drowning in all the dresses I'll buy you.

Regine I can drown myself with what I buy on my own.

Engstrand You need a father's touch, Regine, to guide you by the hand. Listen, I can afford a fine house in Little Harbour Street. It won't empty the pocket. A home for those who wander on the sea. You understand.

Regine I don't want to live with you. I want nothing to do with you. Get away from me.

Engstrand You won't stay with me for long, girl. You'll soon bid your fond farewells. But if you knew how to conduct yourself, you'd do well. These past few years, you've grown into a good-looking girl –

Regine Have I?

Engstrand Before long an officer – maybe even a captain –

Regine I wouldn't marry a man like that. Sailors have no *savoir vivre*.

Engstrand No what?

Regine I know all about the wanderings on the sea. You don't marry that class of people.

Engstrand Don't marry them, then. But all the same, you could make it worth your while.

9

He speaks confidentially.

Himself and your mother – that Englishman – the one who'd got the yacht – six hundred kroner – that's what he paid. And her – no better looking than you, she –

She turns towards him.

Regine Get out.

He retreats.

Engstrand You would never raise your fist against me – I know.

Regine Slander my mother and I will hit you. I said, get out.

She drives him towards the garden door.

Don't slam the door. Young Mr Alving –

Engstrand Is enjoying his sleep, yes. You're hot and bothered about young Mr Alving.

He speaks more quietly.

Tell me this. Would it be him –

Regine Get out now. Don't go that way. Pastor Manders is coming. Get down the kitchen stairs.

He exits right.

Engstrand Talk this business over with him. He's the man to tell you what's due to a father from his child. Because you are my child – I am your father. I can prove that. The parish register.

He exits through the second door which Regine has opened and closed after him.
 She looks hastily in the mirror, fans herself with a handkerchief and straightens her collar.

She then starts busying herself with flowers.
Wearing an overcoat, Pastor Manders enters, carrying an umbrella, with a small travel bag strapped over his shoulders, through the conservatory garden door.

Manders Miss Engstrand, good morning.

She turns around, looking delighted and surprised.

Regine Look who's here! Pastor, good morning. Is the boat in already?

Manders Just arrived.

He enters the garden room.

Hasn't the weather been dreadful, rain.

She follows him.

Regine The farmers are thanking God for this weather, Pastor.

Manders You're right. I'm sure. When you live in the town, you rarely think about that.

He starts taking off his overcoat.

Regine May I help? There. Soaking wet. I'll just hang it up in the hall. The umbrella. I'll open it up to let it dry.

She exits with the things, second door to the right.
Pastor Manders leaves his travelling bag and hat on a chair.
Regine has returned.

Manders It's good to be under a warm roof. How are things progressing here – well?

Regine Thank you – yes.

Manders Hectic – I imagine – because of tomorrow?

Regine Hectic – Still a lot to do.

Manders I hope Mrs Alving is at home?

Regine She is, yes. Upstairs. Preparing cocoa for the young master.

Manders Oswald. Yes. Oswald is supposed to have arrived, I heard tell at the harbour.

Regine The day before yesterday. We'd expected him today, but he arrived the day before yesterday.

Manders Healthy – I hope?

Regine Thank you, yes, he is. Exhausted by the journey. Paris, from Paris he came straight here, the whole journey on the one train. I believe he's asleep just now, so we'd better talk a teensy bit quieter.

Manders Hush, hush – quiet as mice.

Regine adjusts an armchair by the table.

Regine Please sit down, Pastor. Make yourself at home.

He sits down.
She places a footstool under his feet.

There you be. Is that all right?

Manders Perfectly. Perfect. I am sitting splendidly.

He observes her.

Miss Engstrand, do you know what I'm going to tell you? I do think you've grown since I last set eyes on you.

Regine Do you think so, Pastor? Madame say I've filled out as well.

Manders Filled out? A little perhaps – fetching, becoming.

Silence.

Regine Should I perhaps tell Madame you're here?

Manders No rush, thank you, good girl. No rush. My dear Regine, your father – tell me, how is he coping out here?

Regine Doing well, thank you, Pastor.

Manders He called in to see me when he was last in town.

Regine Did he? He's always so pleased when he's spoken to the Pastor.

Manders You see quite a lot of him these days?

Regine Do I? I suppose I do, when I have the time.

Manders Your father, Miss Engstrand, is not the strongest of men. He very much needs a firm hand to guide him.

Regine That may be so, yes.

Manders Someone he can be fond of, someone he can trust. When he last came to see me, he admitted that with all his heart.

Regine He let that slip to me as well. But would Mrs Alving want me to jump ship? – No, definitely not now, when we have the new orphanage to run. I would hate to desert Mrs Alving – she has always been so kind to me.

Manders There is a bond between father and daughter. It is called duty, my dear girl. Your mistress would have to give permission, naturally –

Regine Is it right for a girl my age to keep house for a single man?

Manders Miss Engstrand, we're talking about your father –

Regine That may be. Still, a nice house, belonging to a real gentleman, if that were the case –

Manders My dear Regine –

Regine Someone I could – give my devotion – look up to him – take the place of a daughter almost –

Manders My child, my good dear –

Regine Then I'd like to live in the town. Quite lonely, out here. Alone in the world. You know – the Pastor knows what that means. I can dare say I am willing, and I am wanting. Would you know of any such place for me, Pastor?

Manders I know? I don't. Isn't it dreadful – I really don't.

Regine Just in case – at least think of me, my dear Pastor.

He gets up.

Manders I will, yes, Miss Engstrand. Yes.

Regine Yes, because if I –

Manders Fetch Mrs Alving now, if you would perhaps be kind enough.

Regine She will be here straight away, Pastor.

Manders walks up and down the room a few times, stands upstage for a while with his hands folded behind his back and looks out into the garden.
He then moves near the table to pick up a book.
He looks at the title page, frowns and picks up a few more.

Manders I see.

Mrs Alving enters through the door stage left.

She is followed by Regine, who immediately exits
through the rear door stage right.
Mrs Alving extends her hand.

Mrs Alving Welcome, Pastor Manders.

Manders I'm here as you made me promise. Good
afternoon, Mrs Alving.

Mrs Alving On time as always.

Manders The trouble I had to escape. I sit on so many
blessed committees and boards –

Mrs Alving You have been all the more kind to be so
punctual. We can now dispense with business before
lunch. Your luggage, where is it?

He answers quickly.

Manders My clothes – at the grocer's house. I'll stay
there tonight.

She suppresses a smile.

Mrs Alving No persuading you to spend the night here
with me this time either?

Manders No persuading. Many thanks, but no, all the
same. I'll perch where I usually perch. Handy for when
I need to get back on the boat.

Mrs Alving Have your own way. I do think two old
friends like ourselves –

Manders Have your little joke, God bless you. Look at
you today – ecstatic, naturally. The big celebration
tomorrow and now you have Oswald back home.

Mrs Alving Bliss – you can imagine. It's over two years
since he was last home. Now he's promised to stay with
me for the whole winter.

Manders He has really? A beautiful thing to do – the act of a good son. Living in Rome and Paris, I'd imagine that must be so much more attractive.

Mrs Alving Yes, but you see he has his mother here at home. My own, darling boy, he's devoted to his mother – devoted.

Manders Well, it would be too sad if running away and dabbling in art – that sort of thing – were to corrupt him. Absence has made the heart fonder.

Mrs Alving That's right, yes. There's nothing amiss with him. No. It will really amuse me to see if you can still recognise him. He'll come down shortly. Having a little sleep on the sofa. My dear Pastor, do sit down.

Manders Thank you. Is this a convenient time?

Mrs Alving Of course, yes.

Manders Good. Just let me show you –

He goes to the travel bag on the chair, takes a pile of papers from it, sits down at the opposite end of the table and looks for space to leave the documents.

Now, the first one is –

He interrupts himself.

Mrs Alving, why have you these books here? Tell me.

Mrs Alving Books? They're the books I read.

Manders You read this kind of writing?

Mrs Alving I certainly do.

Manders This kind of writing – you feel – improves you? Makes you more happy?

Mrs Alving I feel more secure – more safe, yes.

Manders Beyond belief. Why?

Mrs Alving These books explain things to me. They confirm what I myself already think. That's what's beyond belief – there's really nothing new in them. They say what most people already know. It's just that some people don't realise it, or don't admit it.

Manders Dear God – you truly believe most people –

Mrs Alving Exactly, yes, I do.

Manders Not in this country, never. Not among our own kind –

Mrs Alving Absolutely, among our kind.

Manders I must say –

Mrs Alving What have you got against these books? Tell me.

Manders Against them? You can't imagine I concern myself with these publications, reading –

Mrs Alving So you don't know what it is you are condemning –

Manders I've read enough about these writings to condemn them.

Mrs Alving Tell me, in your opinion –

Manders My dear Madam, many things in life teach us to rely on others. That's how the world works. And it's just as well. If it didn't, what would happen to society?

Mrs Alving No. No. You may be right there.

Manders I don't deny these writings can have their attractions. I can't condemn you because you wish to know what the world beyond these shores considers to be – what it values, intellectually – you've let your son stray there for so long. But –

Mrs Alving But –

He lowers his voice.

Manders But one keeps that kind of talk to oneself, Mrs Alving. It's not done to tell outsiders what you read and think within the confines of your own four walls.

Mrs Alving Of course not, no – I think that as well.

Manders Think of your duty to this orphanage. You did decide to build it at a time when your opinions on spiritual matters were radically different to what they are now. Entirely different, yes?

Mrs Alving Entirely, yes. I admit that. But the orphanage –

Manders The orphanage – yes. That's what we're supposed to be discussing. So, be cautious, dear Madam. Now, let us go on with business –

He opens a folder and takes out several documents.

You see these?

Mrs Alving The documents?

Manders Every one. All completed. What a terror of a job to finish them in time. I've really had to push. The powers-that-be are terribly conscientious when it comes to making decisions. Still, here we are.

He leafs through the pile.

Registered deed – Solvik farm belonging to the Rosenvald estate – dormitories newly built – classrooms, staff quarters, chapel, listed. The appropriation of the legacy here, and the statutes of the foundations. Look at this –

He reads.

The Articles of Association for the orphanage to be called Captain Alving's Memorial Hall.

Mrs Alving That is it. So.

Manders Captain – I chose that name – more fitting – to his status –

Mrs Alving Yes.

Manders Our kind –

Mrs Alving As you wish – yes, yes.

Manders This is the savings book for the capital that bears the interest, set aside to cover the running costs of the orphanage.

Mrs Alving Thank you. For convenience you hold on to it.

Manders As you please. Let the money stay in the savings bank just now. Not an attractive rate of interest. Four per cent with six months notice. Later we might find a good mortgage deal. A first mortgage, of course – of undisputed security – then we can probe further –

Mrs Alving Pastor Manders, you know best.

Manders I'll keep an eye out. Now something I've wanted to ask many times –

Mrs Alving What?

Manders The orphanage – insured or not?

Mrs Alving It must be insured, of course.

Manders Stop there, Madam – look closer at this matter.

Mrs Alving I insure everything – property, livestock, crops.

Manders On your own estate, naturally. I do the same. This is different. This is an orphanage, dedicated to a higher purpose.

Mrs Alving Even so –

Manders I myself would not find it insulting to safeguard against all eventualities –

Mrs Alving I agree entirely.

Manders But the people out there – what's their feeling? You know them better –

Mrs Alving Feeling?

Manders Are many people of the opinion – people who have a right to hold an opinion – might they take it as an insult?

Mrs Alving What precisely do you mean, entitled to hold an opinion?

Manders I'm thinking of men – independent, influential men – men whose opinions must be given weight.

Mrs Alving There are plenty who might regard it as an insult –

Manders I knew it. Plenty of that type in town. They might draw the conclusion that you and I are lacking in faith, faith in a higher power.

Mrs Alving Well, you know that at least as far as you're concerned –

Manders I know, yes, I know. My conscience is clear, that's true. But we'd not be able to put a stop to a wrong and unpleasant interpretation. That could harm – it could restrict the work of the orphanage.

Mrs Alving If that were the case, then –

Manders And I cannot ignore the awkward – indeed, the embarrassing – position I might be in. The orphanage is a leading topic of conversation among those who matter in the town. It will benefit in its way – the local council can spend less on the poor, it's to be hoped. But for myself. I've been your adviser. I've managed the business side of this matter, they might fall on me, the zealots.

Mrs Alving You can't expose yourself to that, you mustn't –

Manders The attacks in certain papers against me – magazines –

Mrs Alving Pastor Manders, that settles it – enough.

Manders You don't want it insured then?

Mrs Alving No, we'll let it be.

He reclines in his chair.

Manders If an accident should happen – one never knows – would you be able to repair it?

Mrs Alving No. I certainly would not, I can tell you that now.

Manders Mrs Alving, do you realise the scale of responsibility we're taking on?

Mrs Alving Do you think we can do anything else?

Manders No. Nothing else. We can't leave ourselves open to the wrong interpretation, and we've no right to insult the parish.

Mrs Alving You can't, you're a clergyman.

Manders I believe we must have faith that an establishment such as this has luck on its side – I really do. It is special, it is protected.

Mrs Alving We can hope so.

Manders Shall we leave it then, so?

Mrs Alving We shall, yes.

Manders Very well. As you desire.

He notes it down.

No insurance, so.

Mrs Alving Strange you mention this today of all days –

Manders I've often thought of asking you –

Mrs Alving Because yesterday we nearly had a fire there –

Manders What?

Mrs Alving False alarm. Some wood shavings, a blaze, in the carpenter's workshop.

Manders Where Engstrand works?

Mrs Alving They say he's careless with matches, yes. Often.

Manders That man, he has much on his mind. Surrounded by temptations. I hear he's now leading a life without blame, thanks be to God.

Mrs Alving Really? Who says that?

Manders He does himself. And he is an excellent worker –

Mrs Alving As long as he's sober –

Manders That sad failing. He says it's all due to his bad leg. I was quite touched the last time he was in town. He came up to me and he thanked me with all his heart because I got him the job here. That way he could be with Regine.

Mrs Alving He doesn't see much of her.

Manders He talks to her every day, he told me himself.

Mrs Alving That may be so, yes.

Manders He feels he needs a firm hand to restrain him when temptation stalks him. It's what I love about Jacob Engstrand. He comes to you and he's helpless, he admits his frailty. The last time he talked to me, when – Listen, Mrs Alving, if it were absolutely necessary for him to get Regine back again –

She gets up quickly.

Mrs Alving Regine?

Manders You must not prevent it.

Mrs Alving I will indeed prevent it. Anyway, Regine will have her place at the orphanage here.

Manders Take into consideration he is her father –

Mrs Alving I know exactly the kind of father he's been to her. She'll not go to him if I can help it.

He gets up.

Manders Madam, please, no offence intended. You misjudge that poor carpenter. It's as if you are frightened.

She answers more quietly.

Mrs Alving Be that as it may. I've taken Regine in. She will stay here.

She listens.

Pastor Manders, no more talk of this.

Joy lights up her face.

Oswald. Listen – coming down the stairs. We'll think only of him now.

Wearing a light overcoat, his hat in his hand, smoking a large meerschaum pipe, Oswald Alving enters through the door stage left. He stops in the doorway.

Oswald I'm so sorry. I thought you were in the office.

He comes closer.

Pastor, good morning.

Manders stares.

Manders Yes. How strange.

Mrs Alving So, Pastor Manders, what do you think of him?

Manders My – is it really –?

Oswald Yes, Pastor, really – it's the Prodigal Son.

Manders Shall we leave the good book out –

Oswald Have I offended the good book?

Mrs Alving Oswald is remembering the time when you didn't want him to become a painter.

Manders I thought you took a wrong turning, but you proved otherwise.

He shakes his hand.

Welcome, welcome. My dear Oswald – may I call you by your first name?

Oswald What else would you call me?

Manders Excellent. My dear Oswald, what I tried to say – you mustn't think I condemn all artists always. I presume many men in that profession do not stain their souls.

Oswald We can but hope so.

Mrs Alving beams happily.

Mrs Alving I know a man who is without stain, body and soul. Look at him, Pastor Manders.

Oswald wanders across the floor.

Oswald Mother, please.

Manders Quite – certainly. That can't be denied. And you're making a name for yourself. The papers here often mention you very, very approvingly. Yes, that's to say – not too much in them recently.

Oswald is by the flowers.

Oswald I've not turned my hand to the painting much recently.

Mrs Alving Even an artist needs a bit of rest.

Manders I can imagine. Gearing up for a great achievement needs preparation, strength.

Oswald Yes. Is it time to eat yet, Mother?

Mrs Alving Half an hour. Thank God he still has a taste for his food.

Manders A taste for tobacco as well.

Oswald Father's pipe – I found it in the attic and then –

Manders Yes. I've solved it.

Oswald Solved what?

Manders Oswald, standing in the doorway then, the pipe in his mouth – it was as if I saw his father alive again.

Oswald No, really?

Mrs Alving How can you say that? Oswald looks like me.

Manders The corner of his mouth, something about the lips, something that is so like Alving – at least when he's smoking.

Mrs Alving No. He has a clergyman's mouth, Oswald, I think.

Manders Yes, yes, several of my colleagues share a similar look.

Mrs Alving Dear boy, put down the pipe. I don't want smoke in here.

Oswald does so.

Oswald My pleasure. I just wanted to try it. I smoked once as a boy.

Mrs Alving You did?

Oswald Quite small I was. I remember I came to see Father in his room one evening. He was so joyously happy.

Mrs Alving You remember nothing from those years.

Oswald I remember it clearly. He sat me on his lap, he let me smoke the pipe. He said, 'Puff, boy, puff, like a good boy.' I did puff and puff, I was quite pale, I think. Big beads of sweat rolled onto my forehead, and then he laughed, as if he would explode.

Manders That was most unusual.

Mrs Alving Oswald is dreaming, my dear.

Oswald No dream, Mother. You do remember this, don't you? You came in and carried me to the nursery. I was sick and I saw you were crying. Did Father often play those games?

Manders When he was young he was a merry fellow, very lively.

26

Oswald And yet he achieved so much in this life. So good, so useful, though he didn't live to be an old man.

Manders My dear Oswald Alving, you have inherited a good man's name, virile, worthy. I do hope it will spur you on –

Oswald Yes, it ought to –

Manders Well, you've come back to honour him – that is laudable.

Oswald The least I could do for Father.

Mrs Alving And I get to keep him for so long. Even more laudable.

Manders I hear you're staying for the winter.

Oswald I put no end to my stay, Pastor. It's good to be at home, so good.

Mrs Alving beams.

Mrs Alving Yes, isn't it?

Manders looks at Oswald sympathetically.

Manders My dear Oswald, you went out into the world early.

Oswald Early, yes. Perhaps too early.

Mrs Alving No. It does a bright boy good, especially an only child. Stuck at home with Mummy and Daddy – that spoils children. Do not stay at home –

Manders I question that, Mrs Alving. The best place for a child is in his parents' house.

Oswald The Pastor has a point, and I agree.

Manders Look at your own son. We can say this to his face. What's happened to him? He is twenty-six or seven. He's never had the chance to know a proper, family home.

Oswald I beg your pardon, you're in the wrong there, Pastor.

Manders I thought you confined yourself to artistic circles.

Oswald I have.

Manders Younger artists –

Oswald The very same.

Manders Those people, they can't afford a home, a family – most of them –

Oswald They can't afford to marry, most of them, Pastor –

Manders That's what I'm saying.

Oswald But they can have a home. Some do. Very neat homes, very laudable.

Excited, Mrs Alving follows the conversation, nodding, saying nothing.

Manders I'm not talking about bachelors. I mean a home, a family, a man with his wife and his children.

Oswald Or with his children and their mother.

Manders Mother?

Oswald Would you rather he cast their mother aside?

Manders That is not legal, not marriage, that is filth.

Oswald I have found nothing filthy in their way of living.

Manders How can a man – or young woman – reared decently – how can they behave that way – before all – in the eyes of the world?

Oswald What else can they do? He's young, he's an artist – he's poor – she's young, she's poor. To get married costs money. What else –?

Manders I'll tell you what they can do, Mr Alving. Not touch each other, never touch – that's what they should do.

Oswald Do not touch? They're young, their blood's on fire, they're in love, that kind of talk won't get you far with them.

Mrs Alving You won't get far, no.

Manders And this is now tolerated. This is allowed to happen openly.

He turns to Mrs Alving.

I was deeply worried about your son, and did I not have reason? These are pits where filth flourishes – a habit – an addiction –

Oswald Pastor, I'm telling you, I've spent many a Sabbath as guest in such pits –

Manders Sabbath?

Oswald The day of rest and laughter. I've never heard a bad word there, and I've never witnessed a dirty deed. Do you know when I've met up with filth?

Manders I do not, thank God.

Oswald Then it's my privilege to tell you. I've met it when our decent husbands, our respectable fathers wander down on their own to examine us. They did the artist the honour of joining us in our humble dwellings. Those gentlemen could tell us of places and things we never dreamt of.

Manders Are you saying decent men from these parts would –?

Oswald When these decent men return home have you never – never heard them talk about the filth, the growing filth beyond these shores?

Manders Yes, I have –

Mrs Alving And so I have as well.

Oswald Believe every word. They know whereof they speak. Experts. But there is another kind of life out there – beauty – free – wonder – stained so – soiled – soiled by them –

Mrs Alving Oswald, mind – don't excite yourself. Not good.

Oswald No. You're right, Mother. Not healthy for me probably. I'm tired. Damned tired. A little walk. Before lunch. I'm sorry, Pastor. It comes over me all of a sudden, but you wouldn't understand it.

He goes through the second stage door.

Mrs Alving Poor child.

Manders Yes, you're right there. That he should come to this. The Prodigal Son is putting it mildly.

She looks at him and says nothing.

What have you to say to all of this?

Mrs Alving I say everything Oswald spoke was right.

Manders Right? The absence of principles – right?

Mrs Alving Living here alone, I've begun to think like him. Me, I never dared do anything about it. Now, my boy will speak for me.

Manders I pity you, Mrs Alving. But I want to talk seriously to you, no longer as your business manager, nor your adviser. I am not your dead husband's friend. That's not who's standing before you. I am now the priest who stood in front of you when your life was at its loneliest.

Mrs Alving And what does the priest want to tell me?

Manders I want to shake your memory. The time is right. Ten years ago tomorrow your husband died. Tomorrow we unveil the memorial to the dead. I will speak in public tomorrow. Today I will speak alone to you.

Mrs Alving Then speak, priest.

Manders The first year of your marriage do you remember how you stood at the very edge of the pit? You left your husband and home. You raced from your husband. You ran away, Mrs Alving and you would not return to him. He begged, he pleaded and you refused, you fled from him – do you remember?

Mrs Alving And the sorrow – the suffering – that first unbearable year – do you remember? No happiness –

Manders Happiness – in this life – what right have we as humans to happiness? What spirit's possessed you? All we have is our duty that we must do. Your duty was to the man you once chose, the man sacred ties bound you to, Madam.

Mrs Alving The kind of life Alving led then, you knew about it very well. You knew what he was guilty of, what he did and did again.

Manders I know well what he was accused of. If those rumours were true, I'm the last man to approve of him. But you were his wife, and it's not up to you to judge.

You had a duty to bear. The cross you had to carry without complaint. You threw it aside. He was a man on a slippery slope, you kicked him further down it. You abandoned him. You risked your good name. Your reputation. And you risked that of other men as well.

Mrs Alving Other men? One man. That's what you mean.

Manders You turned to me for shelter, that was wrong.

Mrs Alving From our priest? A friend, welcome in our house?

Manders Friend. And only that – thank God I was man enough to show you strength. I led you away from your mad fantasies. The Lord granted me grace to bring you back to the path of duty. I guided you back to the home of your lawful husband.

Mrs Alving You did, yes, Pastor Manders, you certainly did.

Manders And I was an instrument of God's will. I broke you. You bowed down and did your duty, you were obedient and for that the rest of your days have been blessed. Did things not happen, as I foretold you? Didn't Alving turn aside from his evil ways and behave himself? Didn't he live with you and love you, no blame for the rest of his days? Didn't the place prosper because of him? Did he not raise you with him? – You shared all his glory. You were a good wife. You deserve that praise, Mrs Alving. I know. But you now make a second great mistake in your life.

Mrs Alving What are you saying?

Manders You turned your back on your duties as a wife. In the same way now you are turning your back on your duties as a mother.

She makes a sound of pain.

All your life you have followed your own will. Fatal.
You want what is without rule or regulation. You'll break
free from all that binds you. Everything that held you
back you've thrown aside, no care, no consideration.
It was only a burden you could get rid of. You could
do what you wanted. You were a wife but you weren't
happy. So you left your husband. You were a mother but
you didn't want – you got rid of your child and gave that
child away to strangers.

Mrs Alving I did. That's true. What I did. Yes.

Manders And the truth is that you are a stranger to that
child.

Mrs Alving No, I am not.

Manders You are. Yes. You must be. And you've got
him back again, have you not? Your husband – you've
sinned against him. You admit that by building his
memorial down there. Admit you have sinned against
your son as well. Lead him back to the fold. There's still
time. Turn back yourself. Save him. Save yourself. Mrs
Alving, you are a mother who has sinned. There is guilt
on your soul. I tell you this to your face. It is my duty.

Silence.
Mrs Alving speaks slowly, in control.

Mrs Alving Priest, you have spoken. Tomorrow you'll
speak more in public about my husband's memory. I will
say nothing. Now I do want to say something to you,
in the way you have spoken to me.

Manders You want to excuse your actions.

Mrs Alving I just want to speak.

Manders Now?

33

Mrs Alving You led me back to the path of duty – that's what you said, yes? And myself, my husband, we had a life together. A life you know nothing about. From that day on, you never set foot in our house again when there was once a time you visited every day.

Manders Yourself and your husband moved away from the town after that.

Mrs Alving We did. While my husband was alive, you never came out here. You were forced to visit me – business, the orphanage – you got involved in that.

Uncertain, Manders speaks quietly.

Manders Helene, if this is an attack, please consider –

Mrs Alving Your duty, your position, yes. And then I was a wife who bolted. A dangerous woman, headstrong – beware, take care.

Manders Mrs Alving, now that is overdoing –

Mrs Alving Yes, let it pass. You have judged me and my marriage, and what I want to say is that you do not question the received wisdom –

Manders So?

Mrs Alving I want to tell you the truth. I've sworn to myself you'd know it some day. Only you would know it.

Manders What is the truth?

Mrs Alving My husband died as deep in his depravity as he'd lived all his days in his depravity.

Manders fumbles for a chair.

Nineteen years of marriage – depraved – dirty – in his desires – as you knew he was before you married us.

Manders He was young – foolish – he made mistakes – a young man's excesses if you like, yet you call that depraved –

Mrs Alving That was the phrase our doctor employed.

Manders I don't follow.

Mrs Alving No need.

Manders I – my head. Your marriage – your whole life with your husband, it was a lie, a pit –

Mrs Alving You know now.

Manders I cannot believe that. How was it possible – how can you hide something –?

Mrs Alving By fighting against it day after day. I did that. Never stopped. Gave birth to Oswald. I believed Alving had shown signs for the better. That didn't last. The fight got tougher then. Fight for life, fight for death, no one would find out what the father of my child – that kind of man – was like. Alving was charming – charismatic – you know that. Who could think anything but good of him? The kind of man who leads the life he led and keeps his reputation. But Manders, something else you must know – something that will disgust your soul.

Manders More than this?

Mrs Alving I put up with him, but I knew what was happening in secret outside this house. Then the insult, the filth, came within the confines of our own four walls.

Manders What?

Mrs Alving Our own home.

She points towards the first door right.

Where we eat. That's where I first got wind of it. I had something to do in there. The door was not quite closed. Our maid entered from the garden. She had water for the flowers in there. I heard her.

Manders What?

Mrs Alving I heard Captain Alving follow her. I heard him say something to her. And then I heard –

She laughs briefly.

Ringing in my ears, mocking me, destroying me, I heard my maid whispering, 'Let me be, let me go, Monsieur –'

Manders Mrs Alving, nothing – it was –

Mrs Alving I soon found out what was in operation. My husband had his way with the girl. And there was – there were consequences.

Manders In this house? This happened –

Mrs Alving In this house, where I have suffered a great deal. To keep him at home through the evenings – the nights – I became his – became his close companion during the savage nights in his room. Sitting with him there, the happy couple, drinking, celebrating, listening to his deranged, damaged wanderings, taking him with my bare hands, dragging him to the violent bed –

Manders is shaken.

Manders You managed to endure all of this?

Mrs Alving Endure it for my little son. But the last kick in the stomach, the maid – when that happened I swore this must come to an end. I took control of the house. Control of him, and everyone else. You see, I now had a weapon to point at him – he didn't dare open his mouth. That's when Oswald was sent away. He was nearly seven. Starting to notice. Asking questions the way boys do. Manders, I couldn't endure that. This house was poison. He would breathe in the filthy air. That's why I sent him away. You now know why he never set foot inside here for as long as his father lived. No one knows the price I've paid for this.

Manders Your trials have cost you plenty.

Mrs Alving I had my work. I survived. And I can say I have worked hard. The improvements in the property, the big changes, Alving got all the credit – do you think he could lift a finger? Him, lying stretched all day long on a sofa reading an old almanack? I'll tell you this as well. If he had a good day I whipped him into doing something. And it was me who carried the whole burden when he went back on the bottle, roaring in his misery, crying for himself.

Manders And you're building a memorial to this man?

Mrs Alving Guilty conscience – that's how it works, that's its power.

Manders Guilty – what do you mean?

Mrs Alving I'd always imagined the truth would come out and be believed. So the orphanage would destroy all the doubts and rumours.

Manders You've succeeded there, Mrs Alving.

Mrs Alving I had one more reason. I wanted my son, my own Oswald, to inherit nothing from his father.

Manders Alving's money –

Mrs Alving The money I've donated year after year – I've worked this out very carefully – it comes to the exact amount that once made Alving an excellent catch.

Manders I see.

Mrs Alving This was the cost. I didn't want Oswald's hands to touch his money. My son will inherit everything from me. He will.

Oswald Alving enters through the second door stage right.
He has left his hat and overcoat outside.

Good, good boy – are you back?

Oswald This rain – it's eternal – what can one do outside? Lunch is ready, I hear. Good.

Regine comes from the dining room with a parcel.

Regine Madam, this has arrived for you.

She hands it to her.
Mrs Alving looks at Manders.

Mrs Alving I assume these are the songs for the ceremony tomorrow.

Manders Yes?

Regine Lunch is served.

Mrs Alving Good. We'll be in in a minute. I just want to –

She starts to open the parcel.

Regine Would Mr Alving like white or red port?

Oswald Both, Miss Engstrand.

Regine *Bien.* Very well, Mr Alving.

She enters the dining room.

Oswald I suppose I should give a hand opening the bottles.

He too enters the dining room.

The door slides halfway open behind him.

Mrs Alving Yes. The hymns, Pastor Manders – here they are.

Manders has his hands folded.

Manders How will I speak tomorrow with a clear conscience? I –

Mrs Alving You will manage.

He lowers his voice so as not to be heard in the dining room.

Manders We must not cause any offence.

She lowers her voice but speaks firmly.

Mrs Alving No. But then this long, filthy farce will be at an end. From the day after tomorrow I will be rid of the dead in this house. As if they never lived. No one will be here but my boy and his mother.

The sound of a chair falling over in the dining room can be heard simultaneously with Regine's sharp whisper.

Regine (*offstage*) Oswald, are you mad? Let me go, Monsieur.

Mrs Alving starts in terror and makes a sound, like the word 'again'.
She stares like a madwoman at the half-open door. Oswald can be heard coughing and humming. A bottle is opened.

Manders What's wrong – what is it, Mrs Alving?

She is hoarse.

Mrs Alving Ghosts. The two who were there, out there, have come back amongst us.

Manders Regine? She is –

Mrs Alving Regine, yes.

Manders Is she –

Mrs Alving Yes. Come. Say nothing – not a single word.

She grips Pastor Manders' arm and staggers towards the dining room.

Act Two

The same room.
Damp fog still lies heavily across the landscape.
Manders and Mrs Alving enter from the dining room.
Mrs Alving speaks while she is still in the doorway.

Mrs Alving You enjoyed lunch, Pastor? I hope so.

She speaks into the dining room.

Oswald, are you joining the company?

Oswald (*off*) Thank you, no. Outside – I'll walk for a while.

Mrs Alving Good, yes. The rain seems to have stopped.

She closes the door to the dining room and calls into the hall.

Regine?

Regine answers offstage.

Regine Yes, Madam.

Mrs Alving Get down to the ironing room – help them with the garlands.

Regine I will, Madam.

Mrs Alving makes sure that Regine leaves.
She then closes the door.

Manders He can hear nothing in here?

Mrs Alving Not when the door's shut. Anyhow, he's going out.

Manders How did I manage to swallow a bite of that blessed food?

Mrs Alving is restless, but she is controlled.
She walks up and down.

Mrs Alving I feel the same. What are we to do?

Manders What are we to do, yes? I swear to God, I don't know.

Mrs Alving Nothing's happened yet – no harm – I'm sure.

Manders Heaven forbid. But it is not right, this relationship –

Mrs Alving Oswald playing games – another game, I'm sure – rest assured.

Manders I've said I know little about these matters, but it's dreadful, I do think –

Mrs Alving She has to get out of this house. Now. That's clear as daylight.

Manders She must, yes.

Mrs Alving Where will she go? We can't allow her –

Manders She goes home, naturally, to her father.

Mrs Alving Father?

Manders Her – Engstrand is not her – no. My God, how can this be? You have made a dreadful mistake.

Mrs Alving I made no dreadful mistake. Johanna had to tell me everything. Alving could not deny it. All I had to do was hush the whole matter up.

Manders The only thing left to do, I suppose.

Mrs Alving She left the house, Johanna. She did rather well by keeping her mouth shut. She went to town and sorted things out. She met up with an old flame, Engstrand, a carpenter. She let hints drop she wasn't short – she'd earned her wages. I imagine she let him think that a sailor, a foreigner, had made her acquaintance when his boat landed here. Then she and Engstrand tied a rather hasty knot. You yourself married them.

Manders How do I say this? I do remember clearly – Engstrand came and asked to be married. He was a broken man, really, he blamed himself for the intemperance. He and his fiancée were quietly –

Mrs Alving He had to blame himself.

Manders How could he have lied so – and to me? I would never have believed Jacob Engstrand capable of that. I won't mince my words with him now, he can face the music. How much money was the girl given?

Mrs Alving Three hundred kroner.

Manders Three hundred kroner. He married a woman for that. A fallen woman.

Mrs Alving How much should I have married a fallen man for? I agreed –

Manders A fallen man – what are you saying? A man – clean –

Mrs Alving When Alving made his vows, was he more clean than Johanna was when Engstrand agreed to marry her?

Manders Completely different –

Mrs Alving Not remotely different. True, the price was different – three hundred filthy kroner against a filthy fortune – a dowry.

Manders Don't compare two different things. How can you? You followed your heart, and the advice of your nearest and dearest.

She does not look at him.

Mrs Alving My heart had strayed at that time, as you well knew, I believe.

He answers distantly.

Manders If I'd had any idea of this I would not have set foot inside your husband's house each day.

Mrs Alving So it is clear I did not consult my heart?

Manders You did your duty – you consulted your mother, your two aunts.

Mrs Alving That's true. The three of them put their heads together for me. How neat and tidy they made it seem – turning down such a man would be madness. If my mother could rise up from her grave, if she could see what all her plans led to –?

Manders It's nobody's fault what happened. One thing's clear. Your marriage was lawful –

Mrs Alving Law, order. I think there's the source of misery in this world.

Manders That is a sin, Mrs Alving.

Mrs Alving Maybe. But I'll not tie myself down any longer. I want freedom and I must work out how to find it.

Manders What are you saying?

Mrs Alving drums on the windowsill.

Mrs Alving I kept Alving's way of life a secret – I shouldn't have. I daren't do anything else. I did that for myself. I was such a coward.

Manders Coward?

Mrs Alving If the world had found out, they'd have pitied him. He needed his bit of fun when his wife did a runner.

Manders Some justice in saying that.

She looks at him firmly.

Mrs Alving If I were the woman I should be, I'd say to my boy, 'Oswald, listen, your father was depraved.'

Manders Merciful God –

Mrs Alving Tell him everything I've told you. Starting from the beginning.

Manders You're very near to frightening me –

Mrs Alving I know. I frighten myself, thinking of it.

She moves away from the window.

I am such a coward.

Manders You did your duty and you call yourself a coward? A child should honour its parents, love its father and mother – have you forgotten that?

Mrs Alving Spare me your platitudes. Ask out straight. Should Oswald love and honour his father?

Manders You're a mother, he's your son, do you want to destroy him? Destroy his ideals?

Mrs Alving What about the truth?

Manders His ideals? What about –

Mrs Alving His ideals? If I were only not such a coward –

Manders Don't shatter his ideals. You'll pay a hard price. Look closely at Oswald. It's tragic that boy does

45

not have many ideals. But I've learned enough to know his father represents an ideal to him.

Mrs Alving You are right there.

Manders Your letters – you encouraged him to believe –

Mrs Alving I did my bit to duty and respectability. That's why I lied and lied and lied to my boy. Coward – coward – that's what I have been.

Manders Mrs Alving, you let your son cherish an illusion, a happy one – don't diminish that.

Mrs Alving Was it right of me? Still, I won't allow him to carry on with Regine. He mustn't hurt that poor girl.

Manders Good God, that would be wrong.

Mrs Alving If I knew he was serious and it would make him happy –

Manders What then?

Mrs Alving No – not possible. Regine isn't that type.

Manders What do you mean?

Mrs Alving If I were not such an idiotic coward, I'd say to him marry her, or fix something up, whatever you like, but please, no lies.

Manders Merciful God – they'd be legally married. That is hideous, unheard of –

Mrs Alving Unheard? Tell the truth, Pastor Manders. Don't you think in this very place that there are many married couples just as closely related?

Manders I don't understand you at all.

Mrs Alving You do.

Manders You think there is a possibility – Yes, it's dreadful that family life is not all it might be, but the things that you're hinting at – well, no one knows, at least not with certainty. Still, you are a mother and you would allow your –

Mrs Alving I wouldn't – not at any cost. That's what I'm saying. I won't allow it.

Manders Because you are a coward, as you call yourself. But God forbid, such a shocking relationship –

Mrs Alving They say we all spring from such a relationship. And who arranged that it should be so, Pastor Manders?

Manders I will not debate such matters with you, Madam. You are really not in a proper state of mind. A coward –

Mrs Alving I'll tell you what I mean. I am frightened – frightened because there is something inside of me – ghosts – that I can never be rid of.

Manders What did you call them?

Mrs Alving Ghosts. I thought I saw ghosts when I heard Regine and Oswald in there. I'm ready to believe we are all ghosts, Pastor Manders. There's more haunting us than what our father and mother leave behind. Dead thoughts – all kinds – dead beliefs – not alive in us, but still sitting anyway, and we cannot be free. I read a newspaper and I see ghosts creeping between the lines. The whole country must be crawling with ghosts. There must be as many as there are grains of sand. That's why we are frightened – all of us, frightened.

Manders So this is how your reading rewards you – a fine harvest of fear. Those filthy, freethinking, disobedient writings.

Mrs Alving Wrong, my dear Pastor. You are the man who made me think. I want to thank you for that.

Manders Me?

Mrs Alving You, when you forced me to do my duty – you called it my duty. You maintained everything was right and true that I rejected as being abominable. My mind would not allow this. I rebelled. That's when I started to examine every stitch of your teaching. I only wanted to unravel one single knot. But when I managed to pick that apart, it all fell asunder. And then I realised it was all false, a complete fabrication.

He is quiet and shaken.

Manders This is my reward for the hardest fight of my life?

Mrs Alving You should call is your saddest defeat.

Manders Helene, it was my greatest victory – the victory over myself.

Mrs Alving It was a crime against us both.

Manders You came to me distressed and you cried, 'I am here. Take me.' I told you then, 'Go home to your husband – that is the law.' Was that a crime?

Mrs Alving Yes, I think so.

Manders We don't understand each other, neither of us.

Mrs Alving Not any more.

Manders I have always and ever, even in the most secret recess of my mind, only regarded you as another man's wife.

Mrs Alving Is that the truth?

Manders Helene –

48

Mrs Alving How easy to forget what one was like.

Manders Not me. I'm the same as I always was.

She changes the subject.

Mrs Alving Yes, yes. To hell with days gone by. You're up to your ears on boards, committees. And I'm here struggling with ghosts, inside me and outside.

Manders I'll help you beat the ones outside. After the horrifying lesson I've learned today, my conscience will not allow a young, single girl to remain in your house.

Mrs Alving Shouldn't we see she's well provided for – a good marriage, I mean?

Manders Beyond any doubt. I think that's best for her. Regine is now at an age – Look, I know nothing about this, but –

Mrs Alving Regine matured early.

Manders She did, yes, didn't she? I seem to remember when I was preparing for her confirmation she was physically well developed, noticeably so. She needs now to go home. Her father must look after – no, Engstrand is not her – How could he keep the truth hidden from me?

There is a knock on the door to the hall.

Mrs Alving Who's there? Come in.

Wearing his Sunday clothes, Carpenter Engstrand stands in the doorway.

Engstrand I beg your pardon, but –

Manders Aha – yes?

Mrs Alving Is that you, Engstrand?

Engstrand None of the maids were about so I took the great liberty of knocking.

Mrs Alving Come in then. Do you want to talk about something to me?

He enters.

Engstrand No, thank you all the same, I wanted a quick word with the Pastor.

Manders paces.

Manders Yes, I see. So, you wanted to talk to me, did you?

Engstrand Yes, I would be so –

Manders stops in front of him.

Manders May I ask what about?

Engstrand What I wanted to say, Pastor, was that we've all been paid off – thank you very much, Madam. As we've finished up, I thought it would be nice and proper since we worked together like good Christians – well, I thought we should round things off with a little service.

Manders A service? At the orphanage?

Engstrand If the Pastor doesn't think that's right, then –

Manders I do, of course, but –

Engstrand I usually lead a prayer myself in the evenings down there.

Mrs Alving Do you?

Engstrand Time to time. Pray for a little strength. But I'm a poor working man. I don't really have the gift for it. God forgive me, but when I realised that Pastor Manders was here anyway, then –

Manders Look here, Mr Engstrand, I want to ask you one question first. Are you in the right state of mind to be in such a congregation? Is your conscience at peace?

Engstrand God help us, Pastor, conscience is a waste of breath talking about.

Manders It's precisely what we should talk about. What do you say?

Engstrand Conscience? It's a messy business sometimes, that.

Manders At least you own up to that. But tell me this truthfully – what is this about Regine?

Mrs Alving speaks quickly.

Mrs Alving Pastor Manders.

He reassures her.

Manders Let me –

Engstrand Regine? Dear God, you're frightening me.

He looks at Mrs Alving.

Is something the matter with Regine?

Manders We can hope not. I'm talking about you and Regine. You are reputed to be her father, yes?

Engstrand hesitates.

Engstrand Yes – well – the Pastor knows about me and the late Johanna.

Manders Stop playing with the truth. Your late wife told Mrs Alving everything before she left her service.

Engstrand Bless me – she did – did she?

Manders You stand exposed, Engstrand. You've been hiding the truth from me for all these years. Hiding it from me with my blind faith in you, in everything.

Engstrand Yes, it's dreadful, I have.

Manders Engstrand, did I deserve this from you? Have I not always helped you out – advised you – given you a hand as far as I was able? Answer me – have I not?

Engstrand Many a time I would have been in a bad way if I had not had Pastor Manders.

Manders This is my reward. You let me list a lie in the parish register. For several years you lied when you owed me the truth. Your behaviour cannot be defended. From now on we are finished.

Engstrand sighs.

Engstrand I suppose so.

Manders What way could you justify yourself?

Engstrand Should she have gone around digging a deeper pit for herself by talking about it? Maybe the Pastor should try imagining himself in the same state as my late wife –

Manders Me?

Engstrand Dear God, I didn't mean it like that. I only meant if the Pastor found himself disgraced in men's eyes as they say. We're men, Pastor, and we shouldn't judge hard a woman who's weak.

Manders I am not. I'm judging you.

Engstrand May I be allowed to ask the Pastor one tiny question?

Manders Ask it.

Engstrand Is it not right and proper for a man to raise up the fallen?

Manders Of course.

Engstrand Is it not also a man's duty to keep his word?

Manders Certainly, but –

Engstrand The woman had her head turned by this Englishman – or maybe an American or a Russian, who can say? That's when she came to the town. The poor creature had refused me once or twice before. She was a pretty thing, and I had this here dodgy leg. Well, the Pastor himself remembers that I dared go into dance halls full of sailors, filthy drunks, you know yourself. When I wanted to lead them back onto the path of righteousness –

Mrs Alving is at the window.

Mrs Alving Did you?

Manders Engstrand, I know those wicked people threw you down the stairs. You've already reported this incident to me. You can bear your wound with pride.

Engstrand I've no pride, Pastor. What I tried to tell you was that she had confessed all to me. She was crying and gnashing her teeth. I have to tell you, Pastor, my heart was sore for her.

Manders Was it, Engstrand? And what then?

Engstrand I said to her, 'The American, he's wandering across the seven seas. And you have sinned, woman, you are a fallen creature. But Jacob Engstrand, he can stand on his own two feet. He can!' I was trying to speak in parables, Pastor.

Manders I perfectly understand you – continue.

Engstrand I raised her up, I wed her so people would not know how she'd stained herself with foreigners.

Manders You behaved in a beautiful way. I simply can't condone you taking money for –

Engstrand Me – money? Not a penny.

Manders looks questioningly at Mrs Alving.

Manders But –

Engstrand Wait a minute, I remember. She had a few coins. I wouldn't touch it. As I said, the wages of sin, dirty gold or notes or whatever it was – we hurl that at the American. That's what I said. But he'd upped and outed and vanished across the big, bad sea.

Manders He'd vanished then, my dear Engstrand?

Engstrand He had. My wife and I settled that the money be spent rearing the child. And it was. I can account for every single penny.

Manders This changes everything.

Engstrand Pastor, that's how it is. And if I say it myself, I've been a true father to Regine – as far as I was able to – for I am a dreadfully weak man –

Manders My good Engstrand –

Engstrand And if I say myself, I reared the child and lived at peace with her mother, God rest her soul. I was master in my own house, as is written in the Bible. It never entered my head to brag to Pastor Manders that I myself, me too, I'd done a good deed in this world. No, when that's the case as far as Jacob Engstrand's concerned, he keeps his mouth shut. Isn't it dreadful that happens all too rarely? When I visit Pastor Manders all I talk about is weakness and frailty. As I've said before, conscience is a messy business sometimes.

Manders Jacob Engstrand, give me your hand.

Engstrand Dear God, Pastor, but –

Manders No buts.

He shakes his hand.

So be it.

Engstrand And if I were to beg the Pastor for his pardon, humbly, politely –

Manders You? I must beg for your pardon.

Engstrand Lord, no, not at all.

Manders And I do so with all my heart. Son, I am dreadfully sorry. I've misjudged you badly – forgive me. And I could only show you a sign of my sincere regret and good will towards you.

Engstrand Would you do that, Pastor?

Manders With the greatest pleasure –

Engstrand Because something has come up. I'm thinking of starting up a kind of hostel for sailors in the town. I'd use the money I saved out here.

Mrs Alving You are?

Engstrand A kind of sanctuary, yes. There are many temptations for wandering sailors. But I believe in my abode they would almost be under a father's watchful eye.

Manders What do you say to that, Mrs Alving?

Engstrand God knows I don't have a pot of gold to spend, but if I could find a generous hand to help out, then –

Manders Yes, we'll discuss this in more detail. This plan of yours, it appeals to me a great deal. Now go ahead, get everything ready. Light some candles, make everything more cosy. Then we'll spend some instructive time together, my dear Engstrand. I do believe that now you are in the right frame of mind.

Engstrand I think so, yes. Goodbye and thank you, dear Madam. Take care of Regine for me.

He wipes a tear from his eye.

The child of my darling wife. Yes, it's strange, but it's as if she is the beating of my own heart. Yes, she is.

He leaves and exits through the hall.

Manders Well, Mrs Alving, what do you say to that man? We heard a very different story there.

Mrs Alving We did, indeed.

Manders You see how we must be terribly careful not to judge anybody. But what a thrill to learn that we were mistaken. Or do you say something else?

Mrs Alving I say you are a little child, Manders. You will always be a child.

Manders Me?

She puts her hand on his shoulders.

Mrs Alving As I say that, I want to throw my arms around you.

He frees himself.

Manders God bless you, no – too sudden –

She smiles.

Mrs Alving Don't be frightened of me – don't.

Manders is by the table.

Manders Your manner sometimes – it is rash. I'm now going to gather the documents together and put them in my bag.

He does so.

That is that. Now, goodbye. Keep your eyes open when Oswald returns. I'll look in on you again.

He takes his hat and exits through the hall.
   Mrs Alving sighs.
   She looks out the window for a moment, tidies up
a little and is about to enter the dining room.
   She stops, with a low cry, in the doorway.

Mrs Alving Oswald, are you still sitting in there?

He calls from the dining room.

Oswald Just finishing my cigar.

Mrs Alving I thought you'd gone out for a while.

Oswald In this weather?

A glass clinks.
   Mrs Alving lets the door stay open and sits down
with her knitting on the sofa by the window.
   Oswald calls offstage.

Was that Pastor Manders who's just left?

Mrs Alving Yes, he went down to the orphanage.

Oswald Did he?

The decanter clinks again.
   She looks worried.

Mrs Alving Oswald, dear, go easy with that liqueur. It's lethal.

Oswald Good for the dampness.

Mrs Alving Wouldn't you rather sit with me?

Oswald Not allowed to smoke in there.

Mrs Alving Cigars you can smoke, you know that.

Oswald All right, I'll join you. Just a suspicion of a drop more. There.

He enters the living room with his cigar, closing the door.
There is a brief silence.

Where did the Pastor go?

Mrs Alving Down to the orphanage, I've told you.

Oswald You did, that's right.

Mrs Alving Oswald, you shouldn't sit so long at table.

Oswald has his cigar behind his back.

Oswald Cosy, cosy.

He caresses and pats his mother.

Mother. Just think, I've returned home to my mother's table. In my mother's room, eating my mother's good food.

Mrs Alving My good, dear son.

He walks about somewhat impatiently, smoking.

Oswald What else can I do here? I can't work –

Mrs Alving Why can't you?

Oswald This rotten weather, how? The sun – no sun – the whole livelong day.

He crosses the floor.

I'm not able to work –

Mrs Alving Maybe you shouldn't have come home – not such a great idea –

Oswald Yes, but that had to be, Mother.

Mrs Alving Yes. I'd be ten times happier if you were happier to be here, even though it brings *me* great joy –

Oswald Joy?

He stops by the table.

Mother, is it a joy for you that I'm home –?

Mrs Alving A great joy for me.

He crumples a newspaper.

Oswald Whether I'm here or not, it's all the same to you, I imagine.

Mrs Alving Oswald, you have the heart to say that? To your mother?

Oswald You managed to thrive – to live without me in the past, Mother.

Mrs Alving I've lived without you, true, yes.

Silence.
  Twilight slowly sets in.
  He puts down the cigar.
  He stops by Mrs Alving.

Oswald May I sit down next to you on the sofa?

She makes room for him.

Mrs Alving Sit down, do.

He sits.

Oswald Something to tell you, Mother.

She is excited.

Mrs Alving Tell me.

He stares into space.

Oswald I cannot any longer –

Mrs Alving What?

Oswald I cannot bear it.

Mrs Alving What is it?

Oswald Not able to write to you. Write about this. Since I've come home –

She grips his arm.

Mrs Alving Oswald, tell me.

Oswald Yesterday – today as well – I tried to push this out of my mind – let myself go. No use.

She stands up.

Mrs Alving Oswald, tell me the truth.

He pulls her down.

Oswald Sit down, I'll try to tell you. I've mentioned being tired, after the long journey –

Mrs Alving Yes – so?

Oswald There's something wrong with me. I'm tired – like never before.

She wants to get up.

Mrs Alving Oswald, you are not sick.

He pulls her down again.

Oswald Mother, sit down. Please, listen. I am not sick, no, not really. Not what you'd call sick. Mother, my mind is not right, broken – I can't work, never will work –

He throws himself in front of her.
  His hands cover his face as he sobs in her lap.

Mrs Alving Look at me, Oswald. That is not true.

He looks up at her with despair in his eyes.

Oswald Never will work. Never. A dead man, still alive –
that's what I'll be like. Imagine something so hideous.
Mother, imagine –

Mrs Alving My poor son. How did this terrible thing
happen to you?

He sits down again.

Oswald I don't understand – I can't. I've never led a
scandalous life. Never – never – never. Don't think I have,
Mother.

Mrs Alving I never have thought that.

Oswald And then this happens – it happens to me. This
tragedy.

Mrs Alving This will pass, my blessed, dear son. This is
over-work. That's all, believe me.

Oswald I thought that at the start. It's not the case.

Mrs Alving From beginning to end, everything – tell me.

Oswald I will.

Mrs Alving What was the first sign?

Oswald Just after my last visit home, I went back to
Paris – violent pains at the back of my brain – like a ring
of iron tightening round my neck. I felt that's the sore
heads plagued me when I was growing up.

Mrs Alving Yes, yes.

Oswald No, it wasn't. I soon knew that. Not able to work, not able. I'd planned to paint something magnificent. I was not able. The power in my hands – paralysed. I could see nothing – could not concentrate. Everything shifting – everything spinning. Nothing was fixed or formed. I didn't know where to turn. I sent for the doctor. I had to be told the truth.

Mrs Alving What do you mean?

Oswald One of the best doctors there. I had to tell him everything. He questioned me about things – I didn't know why they would matter. I didn't understand, what was he asking –?

Mrs Alving What –

Oswald He said, since you were born, worms have been eating your brain, devouring you. *Vermoulu* –

Mrs Alving What did he mean?

Oswald *Vermoulu*. I didn't understand it either. I said, explain, explain. Then the old bastard said –

He clenches his fist and makes a sound as he gets up slowly.

Mrs Alving What did he say?

Oswald 'The sins of the fathers shall descend on the children.'

Mrs Alving The sins of the fathers –

Oswald I nearly hit him in the mouth –

She crosses the floor.

Mrs Alving The sins of the father –

He smiles sadly.

Oswald What do you say to that? I gave him an absolute guarantee that could not be possible. You think he took any notice? He kept on and on. So, I got your letters, I translated all the things you said about my father –

Mrs Alving What then?

Oswald He had to admit he was wrong. So, he told me the truth. The unbelievable truth. I should have shied away from the happy life I shared with my friends. I could not – I was not able for it. You see, it was my own fault.

Mrs Alving No, Oswald, don't believe that. No –

Oswald He said that was the only way to explain it. That's what is obscene. My life is ruined – for ever. No cure for it. And I brought this on myself. I squandered my life. I wanted to do something in this world. Everything. Now, don't even think about it. Not able to think about it. If I could live my life again – one more chance – not to do what I did –

He collapses, burying his head in the sofa.
Mrs Alving wrings her hands and paces up and down, keeping silent.
Oswald looks up after a while, but continues to lie down, resting on his elbow.

If it had only been the sins of the fathers – something that's not my doing. But it is. I have wasted my happiness, my health. I took my future and turned it to dust. I am so ashamed –

Mrs Alving No, son, you haven't. That is not possible.

She bends over him.

It's not as hideous as you think.

Oswald You do not know –

He leaps up.

Mother, I've brought all this bother on you. I've often wished – hoped you'd not really give a damn about me.

Mrs Alving You're my only son, Oswald. You're all I have in this world. You're all I care for.

He clasps both her hands and kisses them.

Oswald I know that – I do, yes. At home, I see that. That's the roughest thing of all. But now you know all. Don't talk about it any more. I can't think about it for very long at a time.

He goes upstage.

Mother, get me something to drink.

Mrs Alving Drink – you want a drink now?

Oswald Anything. Cold punch – you must have some in the house –

Mrs Alving Oswald, please –

Oswald Don't refuse me, Mother. Please. I need to drown out these thoughts.

He enters the conservatory.

It's so dark in here.

She pulls the bell-cord on the right.

The rain, it never ceases. It goes on week after week. Months on end. No sun, never see the sun. All the times I have been back, I don't remember the sun shining –

Mrs Alving Oswald, you're thinking of leaving me.

Oswald Leaving. I don't think of anything. Can't think of anything.

He continues quietly.

I'm trying not to.

Regine calls from the dining room.

Regine Madam called?

Mrs Alving The lamp – bring it here.

Regine Certainly, Madame. It's lit already.

Mrs Alving goes towards Oswald.

Mrs Alving Oswald, don't be a stranger to me.

Oswald Mother, I'm not –

He moves towards the table.

I think I've told you an awful lot.

Regine brings in the lamp and puts it on the table.

Mrs Alving Regine, bring us in a half-bottle of champagne.

Regine Very well, Madame –

She exits.
Oswald touches Mrs Alving's face.

Oswald Perfect. Mother won't let her little boy go without a drink – I know that.

Mrs Alving How can I let you go without anything from now on? My poor, dear Oswald.

Oswald Mother, is that true?

Mrs Alving True?

Oswald Do you mean it?

Mrs Alving What?

Oswald Not let me go without –

Mrs Alving Oswald –

Oswald Shhh.

Regine brings in a tray with a half-bottle of champagne and two glasses which she places on the table.

Regine Will I open –?

Oswald I'll do it myself, thank you.

Regine exits.
Mrs Alving sits by the table.

Mrs Alving I'll not let you go without – What were you asking?

Oswald First things first –

The cork pops.

One glass, two –

He pours one glass and is about to pour the other one.
Mrs Alving holds her hand over her glass.

Mrs Alving No – not for me, thank you.

Oswald Good – then all for me.

He empties his glass, refills it, empties that as well, then sits down by the table. She is tense.

Mrs Alving Well?

He does not look at her.

Oswald You and Pastor Manders – you looked so odd at lunch – quiet. Tell me –

Mrs Alving You thought so?

66

Oswald Yes. Eating –

There is a brief silence.

Tell me. Regine – what do you think of her?

Mrs Alving Think of her?

Oswald Isn't she magnificent?

Mrs Alving Son, you don't know her as well as I do –

Oswald So?

Mrs Alving Regine lived too long in her own house. I should have rescued her a long time ago.

He fills his glass.

Oswald But, Mother, to look at her – isn't she magnificent to look at?

Mrs Alving Regine has her faults, many faults –

He drinks again.

Oswald So what – so what?

Mrs Alving I am immensely fond of her. I'm responsible for her. I would let no harm come to her. Not for all the world.

He leaps up.

Oswald She can save me – only Regine can save me, Mother.

She gets up.

Mrs Alving What do you mean?

Oswald This suffering – I can't get through this on my own.

Mrs Alving You have your mother, haven't you? She can share it –

Oswald That's what I thought, that's why I came home. It won't work. I see that. It won't work. My life here – I can't bear it.

Mrs Alving Oswald –

Oswald I need somewhere different. I must get away from you. I don't want you to see me.

Mrs Alving Son, you are not well. Oswald, as long as you are sick as you are now –

Oswald The sickness, Mother, if it were only sickness, I'd stay with you. In this world, you are my last friend –

Mrs Alving I am, Oswald. You know that.

He paces relentlessly, struggling to say the words.

Oswald Agon— Regr— Remor— Fear, fear. Die, frighten—

Mrs Alving Fear? Why do you feel this –

Oswald Don't ask me – I don't know – I can't describe it –

She goes stage right and pulls the bell-cord.

What do you want?

Mrs Alving My son – to be happy – that's what I want – not sitting here – pining away.

Regine appears in the doorway.

Champagne – more – a whole bottle.

Regine exits.

Oswald Mother –

68

Mrs Alving Do you think we don't know how to live in the country?

Oswald Look at her – magnificent, yes? She is healthy? Hearty, and healthy, yes?

She sits by the table.

Mrs Alving Oswald, sit down.

He sits down.

Oswald Something you should know, Mother. I need to right a wrong I've done to Regine.

Mrs Alving A wrong?

Oswald I've been a naughty boy. Don't be worried – thoroughly innocent. The last time I was at home –

Mrs Alving Yes?

Oswald She interrogated me about Paris – I told her this and that about down there. One day I just happened to say to her, 'Would you not like to go there?' I remember –

Mrs Alving What?

Oswald She blushed and blushed. Then she said, 'I'd like that, I really would.' So I said, 'Yes, we could do something about that,' or words to that effect.

Mrs Alving Yes?

Oswald I forgot about it, of course. Then, the day before yesterday, I came home, I happened to ask her, 'Are you happy I'm staying at home for so long?'

Mrs Alving Well?

Oswald She looked at me very coldly, and she asked me, 'What about my going to Paris?'

Mrs Alving Going to Paris?

Oswald I got it all out of her. She believed me – seriously, she believed me. She'd kept thinking of me and me alone, she'd started to learn French –

Mrs Alving That's why –

Oswald Mother, I saw this healthy, beautiful, magnificent girl – in front of me – I'd never really paid her any attention till now – but there she was standing, her arms were open, ready to take me –

Mrs Alving Oswald.

Oswald It dawned on me – she could be my salvation – because I saw joy – I saw life in her –

She is puzzled.

Mrs Alving Joy – in life – that is what salvation means?

Regine enters the dining room with a bottle of champagne.

Regine Apologies I took so long. I had to go to the cellar –

She puts the bottle on the table.

Oswald Fetch another glass.

Surprised, she looks at him.

Regine Mr Alving, Madame's glass is here –

Oswald Fetch one for yourself, Regine.

Regine starts and gives Mrs Alving a quick, shy, sideways glance.

Well?

She speaks reluctantly.

Regine Madame, do you wish me to –

Mrs Alving Fetch the glass, Regine.

Regine goes to the dining room and Oswald watches her as she goes.

Oswald The way she walks – have you observed? She knows exactly where she is going.

Mrs Alving Oswald, this isn't going to happen.

Oswald The matter's settled. You can see that. No point fighting it.

Regine enters with an empty glass which she keeps hold of.

Regine, sit down.

Regine looks questioningly at Mrs Alving.

Mrs Alving Do sit down. Oswald, what were you saying about joy and life?

Oswald Yes, Mother, there is joy in leading one's life. You don't know much about it here in this house. I've never felt it here.

Mrs Alving Not when you're with me?

Oswald When I'm home, no. But you don't understand.

Mrs Alving Yes, I think I nearly understand it – now.

Oswald And the joy in working. They're really the same thing. But you know nothing about that either.

Mrs Alving You may be correct, Oswald. Tell me more about it.

Oswald People in these parts have been reared to believe work is a curse. Work is a punishment for sin. Life is a misery – the sooner we're dead the better.

Mrs Alving This vale of tears – that's what we turn into.

Oswald But people beyond this place, they won't hear of that. No one really believes that kind of preaching any more. They know the joy – the bliss – just in being alive. Have you ever noticed, Mother, everything I paint is full of joy, of life? Always joyous, always alive. Light as a Sunday morning, and people whose faces are on fire with joy. That's why staying at home with you scares me.

Mrs Alving Scares – what scares you being here with me?

Oswald I am scared that here everything inside me will turn into dust.

She looks at him hard.

Mrs Alving Do you think that would happen?

Oswald I know it would. You could lead your life here the way people do out there, but even then it wouldn't be the same life.

*Mrs Alving has been listening, excitedly.
She gets up with large, thoughtful eyes.*

Mrs Alving Now I see the connection.

Oswald What do you see?

Mrs Alving I see it for the first time. And now I can speak.

He gets up.

Oswald Mother, I don't understand.

Regine too gets up.

Regine Maybe I should leave?

Mrs Alving No, stay. I can speak now. You'll know everything. Make your choice then. Oswald. Regine.

Oswald The Pastor – keep quiet.

72

Manders enters through the door.

Manders Well, we've had an excellent time down there.

Oswald So have we.

Manders We must give Engstrand a hand with this refuge for sailors. Regine must move there and help him out –

Regine Thank you, no, Pastor –

He notices her for the first time.

Manders What – you here? With a glass in your hand –

She puts down the glass and speaks with a French accent.

Regine *Pardon* –

Oswald Regine is leaving with me, Pastor.

Manders Leaving? With you?

Oswald As my wife – if that's what she wants.

Manders God have mercy –

Regine This is not my doing, Pastor.

Oswald Or she stays here, if I do.

Regine says involuntarily.

Regine Here!

Manders Mrs Alving, you shock me.

Mrs Alving Neither will happen – now I can speak out.

Manders No, you're not going to do that. No.

Mrs Alving I can.

Manders No.

Mrs Alving I will. And no ideals will be shattered.

Oswald What are you hiding from me, Mother?

Regine Madame – listen. People shouting outside.

She goes to the conservatory and looks out.
Oswald moves to the left-hand window.

Oswald What's happening? Where's the light coming from?

Regine shouts.

Regine The orphanage is on fire.

Mrs Alving moves towards the window.

Mrs Alving Fire.

Manders That's not possible. I've just been down there.

Oswald My hat. Where is it? Never mind. Father's orphanage.

Mrs Alving It is blazing. My scarf, Regine.

Manders Horrible. Mrs Alving, this is punishment visited on this house of sin.

Mrs Alving Yes, I'm sure. Regine, come with me.

She and Regine hurry out through the hall.
Manders clasps his hands.

Manders And nothing – nothing – insur— nothing –

He exits the same way.

Act Three

The same room.
  The doors are all open.
  On the table the lamp is still lit.
  Outside it is dark.
  In the background, stage left, there is just a faint glow of fire.
  Her head covered by a large scarf, Mrs Alving looks out, standing in the conservatory.
  Wrapped in a scarf, Regine stands a little behind her.

Mrs Alving Burnt to the ground. Burnt.

Regine The foundations are still blazing.

Mrs Alving Why has Oswald not come home? There's nothing to save.

Regine Maybe I better go down there with his hat?

Mrs Alving He's not even got his hat?

Regine points to the hall.

Regine It's hanging in there.

Mrs Alving Leave it. He must be back by now. I'll take a look for myself.

She exits through the garden door.
  Manders enters from the hall.

Manders Is Mrs Alving here?

Regine She's just gone out to the garden.

Manders This night – this dark, dangerous night –

Regine It's a tragedy, isn't it, Pastor?

Manders Don't speak about it. I daren't think about it.

Regine How did it happen?

Manders Don't ask me, Miss Engstrand. How would I know? Maybe you too are going to – Is it not enough that your father –

Regine Him – What about –?

Manders He has put me through the mill.

Engstrand enters from the hall.

Engstrand Pastor –

Manders, alarmed, turns around.

Manders You – are you still trailing after me?

Engstrand I have to, damn it, yes. Dear Lord, this is a dirty business, Pastor.

Manders paces the floor.

Manders Dreadful, dreadful.

Regine What is?

Engstrand It was all because of the prayers. (*Aside to Regine.*) Child, he is ours for the taking. (*Continuing in full voice.*) And I'm the man responsible for the Pastor being blamed for this carry-on.

Manders Engstrand, I assure you –

Engstrand Pastor, you and you alone touched the candles down there, you put a match –

Manders stops pacing.

Manders We have your word alone for that. I have no memory of touching the candles.

Engstrand I saw it with my own two eyes. Pastor, how you took the candle, you snuffed it out, you threw the wick into the wood shavings.

Manders You watched that?

Engstrand I watched it all, I saw.

Manders It's beyond belief. I do not – absolutely do not snuff out candles with my fingers.

Engstrand It did look a bit dangerous, didn't it?

He paces, troubled.

Manders Don't be asking me, stop –

Engstrand moves towards him.

Engstrand And you have not insured it, have you, Pastor?

Manders No. You heard that. No.

Engstrand follows Manders as he continues pacing.

Engstrand No insurance. And then he goes and puts a match to the whole shebang. God above, a bad business.

Manders wipes sweat from his brow.

Manders You can say that again, Engstrand.

Engstrand And this happened to a charity that would benefit the whole district. That's what they were saying. I imagine the papers will be out for your blood, Pastor.

Manders That's what I am thinking. That's the worst of it all. Hating me – accusing me – attacking me. I can't face it – I can't.

Mrs Alving enters from the garden.

Mrs Alving I can't persuade him to leave the fire.

Manders Madam, there you are.

Mrs Alving You were spared delivering your speech, Pastor.

Manders I would have been delighted –

Mrs Alving answers quietly.

Mrs Alving All for the best. The orphanage was neither benefit nor blessing –

Manders You think not?

Mrs Alving You do?

Manders A tragedy, an absolute tragedy for all concerned.

Mrs Alving A business loss – nothing more, nothing less. Are you waiting for the Pastor, Engstrand?

Engstrand is in the doorway to the hall.

Engstrand I am, yes.

Mrs Alving Sit down a while.

Engstrand Thanks, I am happy standing on my feet.

She turns to Manders.

Mrs Alving I presume you'll be leaving on the boat.

Manders It leaves in an hour, I'll –

Mrs Alving Take all the documents with you, if you'd be so kind. No more about this business. I have other things on my mind.

Manders Mrs Alving –

Mrs Alving You will shortly receive a letter giving you authority to settle everything as you deem fit.

Manders Privileged to do just that. There were clear indications as to how the legacy was to be used. These now have, sadly, got to be changed. Completely changed.

Mrs Alving That goes without saying.

Manders Right. For the time being, I'll organise it so that Solvik farm – it will go to the parish. There's a bit of value in the land. Someone will find a use for it. There's a chance I could use the interest – give a hand to some other scheme that might benefit the town.

Mrs Alving Do what you want to do. It's not my concern.

Engstrand Pastor, my little concern – the sailors' hostel –

Manders You have a point there, well worth considering.

Engstrand To hell with considering – No, no, forgive me.

Manders sighs.

Manders I have no idea how long these deliberations will occupy me. Public opinion might demand I relinquish the post. There'll be an inquiry about the fire. It all depends on how that turns out.

Mrs Alving What are you saying?

Manders No one can predict what that outcome will be.

Engstrand moves closer.

Engstrand You most definitely can. I'm here – Jacob Engstrand is here.

Manders Yes, but –

Engstrand speaks more quietly.

Engstrand Jacob Engstrand is not the lad to kick a man who's done him a good turn, not when that same good man is up to his neck in it, they say.

Manders Indeed, yes, but how, my dear –

Engstrand Pastor, your good angel, here to save you, me, you know that.

Manders No – I fear – no – I cannot allow that.

Engstrand That's the way it will be. I know a man who's stood accused before, many times, and he's shouldered that blame.

Manders Jacob.

He presses Engstrand's hand.

You are a rare being. Trust me – all the help you need for your refuge, you will get it from me.

Engstrand wants to thank him but is overcome with gratitude. Manders flings his bag over his shoulder.

Let us depart. The two of us will travel in the one direction.

At the door to the dining room, Engstrand speaks quietly to Regine.

Engstrand Come on, girl, come with me. We'll be the yolk in the egg, that tight, you and me. That's how we'll live.

Regine tosses her head.

Regine *Merci.*

She goes into the hall to fetch the Pastor's travelling clothes.

Mrs Alving Goodbye, Manders.

She goes to where she sees Oswald enter through the garden door.
   Engstrand and Regine help the Pastor on with his overcoat.

Engstrand Right, daughter, goodbye. If you change your mind, you know where to find Jacob Engstrand.

He whispers.

Little Harbour Street, you know.

He turns to Mrs Alving and Manders.

Captain Alving's Home – that's what I'll christen my house for those at peril on the sea. And if I can run it my way, it will be a fitting monument to the late gentleman himself.

Manders is in the doorway.

Manders Yes – yes, come along, my dear Engstrand. Farewell, farewell.

He and Engstrand exit through the hall.
Oswald moves towards the table.

Oswald What house – what is he talking about?

Mrs Alving Some sort of shelter – himself and Pastor Manders, they'll build it.

Oswald It will burn to the ground, just like all of this.

Mrs Alving Why say that?

Oswald Everything will burn – nothing left of my father – nothing to remember. I'm burning, burning –

Regine, puzzled, looks at him.

Mrs Alving Poor Oswald – you stayed down there too long –

Oswald sits by the table.

Oswald Yes, right, maybe so – you might be –

Mrs Alving Your face – it's wet – let me wipe it, Oswald.

She dries his face with her handkerchief.
Indifferent he stares into the air.

Oswald Mother – thank you.

Mrs Alving Are you not exhausted?

He is afraid.

Oswald Sleep? No. I never sleep. I pretend, that's all.
Time enough to sleep.

She looks at him, worried.

Mrs Alving You are sick after all, my dear, good boy.

Regine is tense.

Regine Is Mr Alving not well?

Oswald is impatient.

Oswald Slam the doors shut, all of them. I have this
deadly fear.

Mrs Alving Regine, shut the doors.

Regine shuts the doors and remains in the doorway.
Mrs Alving takes off her scarf.
Regine does likewise.
Mrs Alving pulls a chair near to Oswald and sits
by him.

There, I'll sit beside you now.

Oswald Do, please. Regine, she's to stay beside me as
well. Stay beside me always, Regine. Give me a helping
hand, Regine, won't you?

Regine I don't follow –

Mrs Alving A helping hand?

Oswald Yes, when it's needed.

Mrs Alving You have your mother's hand to help you, Oswald.

Oswald You?

He smiles.

No – the hand I need to help me. No, Mother – you won't give me that.

He laughs sadly.

But then, you are my dearest and my nearest –

He changes tone violently.

Regine, why are you a stranger to me? Why call me Mr Alving? Why do you not say Oswald?

Regine is subdued.

Regine Madame would not approve of that, I'm certain –

Mrs Alving You can – soon. Sit beside us, you as well.

Quietly, reluctantly, she sits on the other side of the table.

You are a troubled man, son. I can lift the weight of the world from you.

Oswald You, Mother?

Mrs Alving Remorse, anger, blame – your poor mind –

Oswald You believe you can do that?

Mrs Alving I can now, Oswald, yes. When you talk about joy – about life – it's as if I saw my own life so clearly all of a sudden.

He shakes his head.

Oswald I understand nothing about this.

Mrs Alving Your father, when he was young, a lieutenant, you should have known him then. Full of life, full of joy.

Oswald I know, yes.

Mrs Alving Looking at him was like Sunday morning. His grace – his goodness – the sheer power of his strength – nothing was going to get in his way.

Oswald And then?

Mrs Alving This boy – young boy – like a child then – he was sentenced to life in this small town, and it had nothing to offer him. Joyless, mindless pleasure, that was it. He worked but it had no worth. He'd go through the motions as if they meant something. He offered his heart and soul – they gave him a desk in an office. He did not have one single friend to share his dreams, who knew what life really meant. Lie about, laze around, that was their way –

Oswald Mother –

Mrs Alving What had to happen, happened.

Oswald What?

Mrs Alving You said it this evening, what would happen if you stayed at home.

Oswald Are you saying my father –

Mrs Alving Your father lost himself looking for something to do. He lost what he loved. And when I came into his home, it was not Sunday that I brought.

Oswald You failed?

Mrs Alving I had duty upon duty drummed into me, and I believed all I was taught for a long, long time. It all came down to duty – one duty after another – mine, his duty, and – Oswald, I turned your father's home into his hell.

Oswald Why did you never write and tell me this?

Mrs Alving I couldn't touch on this till now because you were his son – that's how I look on it –

Oswald How did you look at it then?

She answers slowly.

Mrs Alving I saw one thing only. Before you were born your father was a broken man.

He makes a quiet sound, gets up and goes to the window.

And day in, day out, I thought one thing only. Regine belonged in this house, as much as my own son did.

He turns quickly.

Oswald Regine.

Regine stands up and asks in a subdued way.

Regine I am –?

Mrs Alving You both know now.

Oswald Regine.

Regine speaks to herself.

Regine My mother was – a woman, like that. So.

Mrs Alving Regine, your mother did her best, a good –

Regine Woman, but she was a mother like that. I did wonder, I did, but still – Madam, may I leave now – this instant? Do I have your permission?

Mrs Alving Is that what you really want, Regine?

Regine It really is, yes. Yes.

Mrs Alving You'll do what you want, that's in your nature, but –

Oswald walks towards Regine.

Oswald Leave now? You belong here.

Regine *Merci*, Mr Alving – no, Oswald, now I can say Oswald. It's not how I wanted to say your name –

Mrs Alving Regine, I have not always been honest with you –

Regine No, it would be – a pity – to say you were. If I'd known Oswald was not well, maybe – Nothing worth having can happen now. Not between us. No, I can't stay here, stuck out in the middle of nowhere. I can't be worn out to the bone for the sake of sick people.

Oswald Not even for your next of kin?

Regine Especially not for my next of kin. A poor girl who has her looks must use them. Before you know it, she'll be left skint. No – there's a bit of joy in me, Madam. I have a life to lead –

Mrs Alving Yes, unfortunately. Don't throw yourself away, Regine.

Regine What will be will be. If Oswald is his father's son, then am I not my mother's daughter? So be it. May I inquire of Madam if Pastor Manders knows about me?

Mrs Alving Pastor Manders knows everything.

Regine busies herself with her scarf.

Regine Right – get out of this house, get on the boat now. The Pastor is a kind man to do business with. And I think I've as much right to the money as he has – that filth, my father, the carpenter.

Mrs Alving You're welcome to it, Regine.

Regine fixes her gaze upon her.

Regine Madam could have reared me to be the child of a respectable man. That would have suited me down to earth.

She tosses her head.

Who cares? It's all the same.

She gives a bitter look at the unopened bottle of champagne.

Champagne – I'll get to down it with respectable people soon enough, and drink it as if there were no tomorrow.

Mrs Alving If you need a roof over your head, Regine, come to me.

Regine No. Thank you, Madam. Very much. I do believe Pastor Manders will provide for me. And if that is not to be, I know a house where I belong.

Mrs Alving Where?

Regine A refuge for sailors – Captain Alving's shelter –

Mrs Alving Regine, no, I see what will happen – you will be eaten alive –

Regine Alive? *Adieu* – to God I leave you.

She takes her leave and exits through the hall. Oswald stands by the window.

Oswald Did she leave?

Mrs Alving Yes.

He mumbles to himself.

Oswald It was wrong, this, I think.

Mrs Alving goes behind him and puts her hands on his shoulders.

Mrs Alving Oswald – has this hurt you – shocked you, my dear?

He faces her.

Oswald My father – is that what you mean?

Mrs Alving Your father – who was not happy. Yes. Has it taken too much out of you? I'm so frightened it might have.

Oswald You think that – how? It came as a shock – a deep shock, naturally. But it's really all the same to me.

She pulls her hands away.

Mrs Alving The same? Your father's heart was broken – beyond repair –

Oswald My heart goes out to him, naturally, as it would to anyone –

Mrs Alving He was your father. That makes an almighty difference.

Oswald Father. Yes, father. I know damn all about my father. Never have. I remember one thing only. He once made me sick – he made me vomit.

Mrs Alving Terrible to think about that. A son should love his father – no matter what –

Oswald When the son has nothing to thank his father for? The child never knew his father. Why should he love him? You pride yourself on being so well informed – do you really believe in that old wives' tale?

Mrs Alving An old wives' tale?

88

Oswald Exactly. Mother, you know that it is. Just words in the wind, blown hither and thither.

Mrs Alving Ghosts.

She is shaken.
  Oswald crosses the floor.

Oswald Ghosts. Call them ghosts.

She cries out.

Mrs Alving Oswald, you don't love me, as he did not love me.

Oswald At least I know you.

Mrs Alving Know me – but that's all.

Oswald I know how much you care about me. I should be grateful for that, I suppose. Now you can be useful to me, when I am not well.

Mrs Alving I can, can't I, Oswald? You illness has brought you home to me. I could almost bless it. I see now you're not mine yet. I have to win you.

Oswald That is all just talk. You have to remember, Mother – I am not well. I can't worry about others. I have enough to do thinking about myself.

She is subdued and patient.

Mrs Alving I will be meek and I will be mild.

Oswald Then, Mother, you'll be happy.

Mrs Alving You're right, son, yes.

She goes towards him.

Have I removed all your blame, and your remorse?

Oswald You have. Who's going to remove the fear?

Mrs Alving Fear?

He crosses the floor.

Oswald Regine would have done it – she would have felt no fear.

Mrs Alving Regine? I don't understand –

Oswald Late into the night, isn't it, Mother?

Mrs Alving Early in the morning.

She looks out into the conservatory.

Day's breaking over the mountains. The sky will clear, Oswald. You'll see the sun.

Oswald I would like that. I have to live, I have much to look forward –

Mrs Alving I'd think so.

Oswald If I can't work –

Mrs Alving You'll be working again – soon. You will. You have nothing to brood about – you can stop tearing yourself to pieces –

Oswald You knocked all the nonsense out of me. Good. When I get over this one thing, when I –

He sits down on the sofa.

Mother, talk to me.

Mrs Alving Yes, talk.

She pulls an armchair towards the sofa and sits close by him.

Oswald And the sun will rise. In time. And this fear – I won't feel it any more. You'll know –

Mrs Alving What will I know – what are you saying?

He is not listening to her.

Oswald Mother? If I asked you to do anything, you said this evening you'd do it, didn't you?

Mrs Alving Yes, I did. Yes.

Oswald You'll stand by that?

Mrs Alving I'll stand by that. Rely on me. I live for you, and only you.

Oswald Yes. Listen to this – listen. Your mind, Mother, is tough. I know that. Now sit very still, listen, you have to.

Mrs Alving Oswald – Oswald –

Oswald Don't shout. Are you listening? Promise me that? Sit still and talk. Promise me, Mother?

Mrs Alving Promise. Talk. Yes.

Oswald Right. Know – this tiredness – worn to the bone – work – I can't – think about work – It's not in itself the disease –

Mrs Alving What is the disease?

Oswald My father – my disease – in here.

He points to his forehead.

Mrs Alving Oswald –

She is almost speechless.

Oswald Here –

Mrs Alving No –

Oswald In here –

Mrs Alving No.

Oswald Don't raise your voice. I can't endure that. It's stuck in here. It's waiting. Do you see that? Any time it can explode.

Mrs Alving moans like a wounded animal.

Calm. Please. That's how I am.

She leaps up.

Mrs Alving Not true. Not possible. Oswald. Not so. Not –

Oswald Away from here, I had one fit. It passed. Soon. Then I knew what had happened, and the fear – the ghosts – began to haunt me, so I came back to you as soon as I could.

Mrs Alving So that is what you fear –

Oswald Because it is putrid – filthy. Another deadly disease I could face – I'm not afraid of dying, but I want to live as long as I can.

Mrs Alving You have to, Oswald – you have to.

Oswald But it is filthy. Ba-ba – Mama, ba-ba again. Fed. Have to be fed – cleaned – filth –

Mrs Alving The child needs his mother –

Oswald Filth –

Mrs Alving She will take care of him.

Oswald Don't want that – never wanted that. Filthy – filth – year after year. A ghost of an old man. And if you die before me, then –

He sits in Mrs Alving's chair.

It might not happen quickly. The doctor said. He said the brain softens. Softens the brain.

He smiles softly.

Isn't that beautiful? I always think of velvet, cherry red, curtains, something delicate to stroke.

She screams.

Mrs Alving Oswald.

He leaps up again and crosses the floor.

Oswald Regine – you've stolen her from me. I wish I'd still had her. She would have helped me – given me her hand –

She goes to him.

Mrs Alving Son, what are you saying? Would I not give you any helping hand you need –

Oswald That fit I had, when I got better the doctor told me it would come back – it would definitely come back – there would be no hope then –

Mrs Alving He was heartless enough –

Oswald I insisted he tell me. I told him I had to make arrangements.

He gives a cunning smile.

And I have.

He pulls a little box out of his breast pocket.

See this, Mother?

Mrs Alving What is it?

Oswald Morphine.

Mrs Alving Oswald.

Oswald Morphine.

Mrs Alving Son.

Oswald Twelve capsules of morphine.

Mrs Alving Oswald, give me the box.

She reaches for the box.
  He hides it in his pocket.

Oswald Wait, Mother.

Mrs Alving I cannot survive this.

Oswald You will live, you have to. If Regine – if I'd had Regine here – she would have helped me – when I told her how I am – the finishing touch, she would have – I'm sure –

Mrs Alving No – never.

Oswald When she saw this thing possess me, lying there – a baby – can't do anything – powerless, lost – little – no God left to help me –

Mrs Alving Regine would never have helped you – not for all the world –

Oswald Regine would have done it. She knows how to enjoy life. She would not waste her days caring for damaged goods like me.

Mrs Alving Thank God Regine is not here.

Oswald You are, Mother. You will have to help me. Help me.

She screams.

Mrs Alving I am your mother.

Oswald Help me because you are my mother.

Mrs Alving I gave life to you.

Oswald And I did not ask you for my life. What kind of life have you given me? I give it back to you. I don't want it. You have to take it.

Mrs Alving Help me.

She runs into the hall.

Help me.

He follows her.

Oswald Don't leave me. Where are you going?

She is in the hall.

Mrs Alving For help. A doctor. Let me leave, Oswald.

He is in the same place.

Oswald You are not leaving. No one will come in here.

Mrs Alving Oswald.

A key is turned.

Oswald.

She enters.

My child.

He follows her.

Oswald Do you love me, Mother? Can you watch me be so frightened? Watch me suffering so?

There is a moment's silence.
Then Mrs Alving speaks, in complete control.

Mrs Alving Here is my hand.

Oswald You will –

Mrs Alving If I have to. But I will not have to. That is not possible.

Oswald Yes, let's hope so. We'll live together now as long as we can. Mother, thank you.

He sits down in the armchair.
Mrs Alving has moved to the sofa.
Day breaks.
The lamp on the table is still burning.
Cautiously, she moves closer.

Mrs Alving Calm? You feel –

Oswald Yes.

She moves slowly to him.

Mrs Alving You were imagining things, Oswald. Filthy things. You just imagined them. The shock – you weren't able for the shock. That's what happened. Rest. You're home now – you have your mother. My good son. What do you want? Point to it and it's yours, just like when you were a little boy. See. It's passed, the panic. Easy as pie. Easy. I knew that. Do you see, Oswald? The sun is shining brightly. This lovely day we'll have. Now you can see your home.

She goes to the table and puts out the lamp.
The sun rises.
In the background the glacier and the peaks gleam in the light of the sun.
Oswald sits in the armchair, his face turned from what is happening behind him.
He says, all of a sudden.

Oswald Sun. Give. Mother. Me.

Puzzled, at the table, Mrs Alving looks at him.

Mrs Alving What do you say?

Heavily and without hesitation, he says:

Oswald Sun. Sun.

She moves towards him.

Mrs Alving What is wrong, Oswald?

He appears to dwindle in the chair.
All his muscles paralyse.
His face loses all expression.
His eyes are apathy, staring into the air.
She is trembling with terror.

What's happening?

She screams in terror.

Oswald – Oswald –

She throws herself on her knees.
She shakes him violently.

Look at me, Oswald. Do you not know your mother?

He speaks as flatly as before.

Oswald Sun. Sun.

She leaps up in despair.
She tears at her hair.
She screams.

Mrs Alving This is not happening.

She whispers as if paralysed.

This is not happening. Never – never –

She speaks suddenly.

Where did he hide them?

Rapidly, she fumbles across his chest.

Ghosts.

She retreats a few paces and screams.

No.

Pause.

No.

Pause.

No. Yes.

Pause.

No. No.

She stands a few steps away from him.
   Her hands tangle her hair.
   She stares at him.
   She is in terror, without speech.
   He sits motionless, as before.

Oswald Sun. Sun –